J B Irwin
Gagne, Tammy
Day by day with Bindi Sue Irwin /

RANDY'S CORNER

DAY BY DAY WITH...

BINDI SUE IRWIN

BY
TAMMY GAGNE

Mitchell Lane
PUBLISHERS

P.O. Box 196
Hockessin, Delaware 19707
Visit us on the web: www.mitchelllane.com
Comments? Email us:
mitchelllane@mitchelllane.com

Printing   1   2   3   4   5   6   7   8   9

RANDY'S CORNER

DAY BY DAY WITH. . .

Beyoncé	Mia Hamm
Bindi Sue Irwin	Miley Cyrus
Chloë Moretz	Selena Gomez
Dwayne "The Rock" Johnson	Shaun White
Eli Manning	Stephen Hillenburg
Justin Bieber	Taylor Swift
LeBron James	Willow Smith

Library of Congress Cataloging-in-Publication Data
Gagne, Tammy.
 Day by day with Bindi Sue Irwin / by Tammy Gagne.
    p. cm. — (Randy's corner)
Includes bibliographical references and index.
 ISBN 978-1-61228-326-5 (library bound)
1. Irwin, Bindi, 1998– —Juvenile literature. 2. Wildlife conservationists—Australia—Biography—Juvenile literature. 3. Herpetologists—Australia—Biography—Juvenile literature. 4. Television personalities—Australia—Biography—Juvenile literature. I. Title.
QL31.I77G34 2013
597.9092—dc23
[B]
                                                                                    2012018310
eBook ISBN: 9781612283951

ABOUT THE AUTHOR: Tammy Gagne has written dozens of books for children, including *Day by Day with Justin Bieber* and *What It's Like to Be Oscar De La Hoya*. One of her favorite pastimes is visiting schools to speak to kids about the writing process.

DAY BY DAY WITH

BINDI SUE IRWIN

Kids all over the world play with stuffed animals. Some have a favorite toy elephant, koala, or even a crocodile. For Bindi Irwin, these animals—the real ones—have been a big part of her life from the beginning.

Bindi is an actress, a television host, and a dedicated conservationist. Protecting wild animals and their habitats runs in the Irwin family. Bindi's mother, Terri Irwin, runs the Australia Zoo in Queensland, Australia. Bindi's father, Steve Irwin, was the famous "Crocodile Hunter" from the television series of the same name.

Australia Zoo

Home of The
Crocodile Hunter

Steve and Terri met in 1991 when she visited the zoo he ran with his parents in Australia. Terri was a zoologist from the United States who worked with lots of different animals. She was in Australia trying to find new homes for cougars, but what she found there was a new home of her own. "It was love at first sight," she told Animal Planet. She and Steve got married the next year.

On July 24, 1998, the Irwins had their first
child, a little girl. They named her Bindi.
Steve and Terri first heard the name Bindi
while working with the Kalkadoon
Aborigines. The Kalkadoon
Aborigines are a tribe of people
who live in Queensland,
Australia.

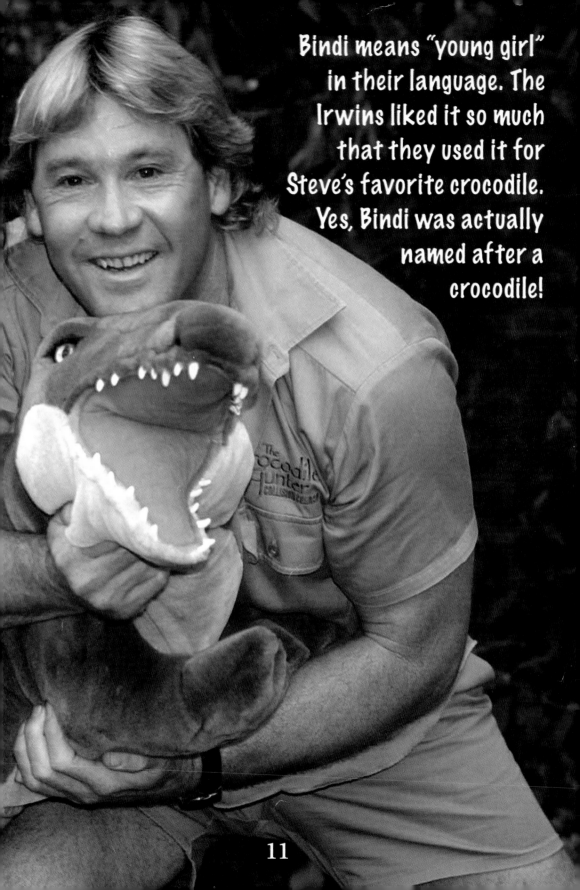

Bindi means "young girl" in their language. The Irwins liked it so much that they used it for Steve's favorite crocodile. Yes, Bindi was actually named after a crocodile!

Bindi had her own Burmese pythons before she was two years old. Terri says that she used to kiss them and carry them around with her. When she got older, Bindi told ABC 4 Kids, "I really love snakes and crocodiles, but my favourite animal is my pet rat, Candy . . . We go out rollerblading and he rides on my shoulder. He likes to play with all of my other animal friends too, except the snakes, of course!"

Many kids find snakes and crocodiles scary, but Bindi doesn't see them this way at all. She told ABC 4 Kids, "I have been around all types of animals since the day I was born. My dad taught me to respect all animals so I've never had to overcome any fear. Plus, I'm always with someone who knows the safe way to interact with these animals."

In 2003, the Irwins welcomed their second child, a son. They named Bindi's baby brother Robert.

When she was only eight years old, Bindi began working on her own television show. *Bindi the Jungle Girl* aired on Discovery Kids from 2007 until 2008. The show was set in a huge tree house that most kids would call a dream house instead. In each episode, Bindi would teach viewers about different kinds of wild animals.

In 2006, tragedy struck the Irwin family. While Steve was filming underwater at the Great Barrier Reef, he was pierced in the chest by a stingray's barb. Steve was killed instantly. At the memorial for her father, Bindi got the chance to talk about him. She said, "I don't want Daddy's passion to ever end. I want to help endangered wildlife just like he did. I had the best Daddy in the whole world and I will miss him every day."

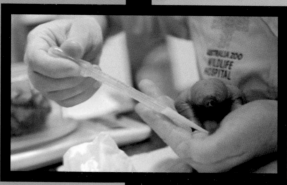

Many people call Bindi a "chip off the old croc," meaning that she is a lot like her father. "I'm going to become a wildlife warrior just like he was," she has said. Bindi has already done that and so much more!

THE AUSTRALIA ZOO'S WILDLIFE WARRIORS READATHON ENCOURAGES KIDS TO DO TWO IMPORTANT THINGS: READ BOOKS AND HELP RAISE MONEY TO CARE FOR ANIMALS, LIKE PUGGLES. A PUGGLE IS A BABY ECHIDNA (PRONOUNCED IH-KID-NA), AN UNUSUAL ANIMAL FOUND IN AUSTRALIA, TASMANIA, AND NEW GUINEA.

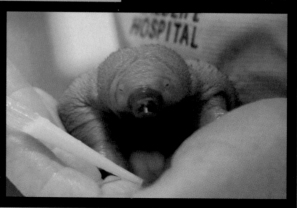

BINDI AND SENIOR NURSE AND REHABILITATION COORDINATOR VICKY TOOMEY POSE WITH MUGGLES, A PUGGLE AT THE AUSTRALIA ZOO WILDLIFE HOSPITAL.

In addition to her television show, Bindi has also starred in a major motion picture—*Free Willy: Escape from Pirate's Cove.* Her character in the film, Kirra, was a young girl on a mission to save an orca whale.

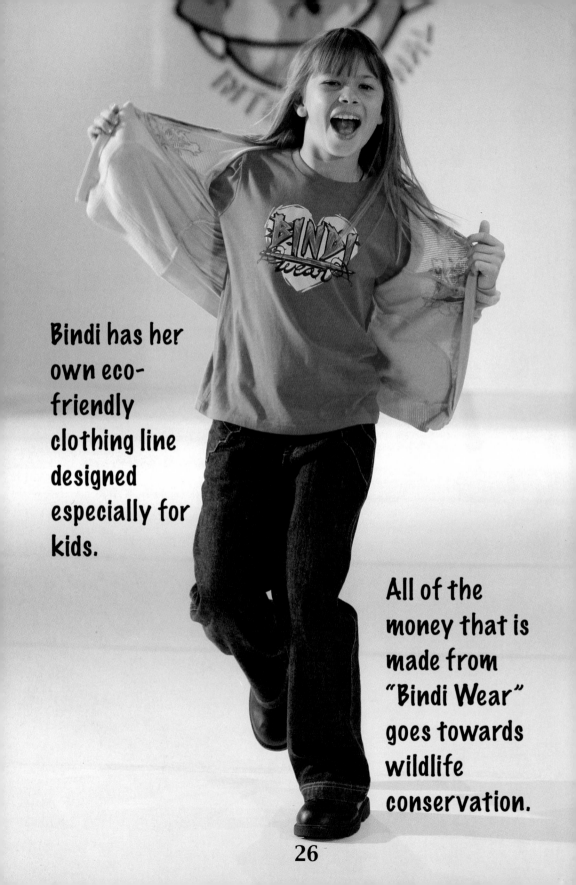

Bindi has her own eco-friendly clothing line designed especially for kids.

All of the money that is made from "Bindi Wear" goes towards wildlife conservation.

In 2008, Wild Republic created a talking Bindi Irwin doll, along with a line of stuffed animals.

And if all that wasn't enough, Bindi has even become an author. Her series of children's books are stories of adventures that take place at the family's zoo.

In 2012, Bindi turned fourteen. With many teenage years ahead of her, she is sure to do even more exciting and meaningful things. As she does, the memory of her father is always near. "He inspires me," she shares with *People*. "I keep him with me the whole time."

FURTHER READING

BOOKS

Breguet, Amy E. *Conservation Heroes: Steve and Bindi Irwin*. New York: Chelsea House, 2011.

Irwin, Bindi and Chris Kunz. *Bindi Wildlife Adventures*. Naperville, Illinois: Sourcebooks Jabberwocky, 2011.

Tieck, Sarah. *Bindi Irwin*. Minneapolis, MN: ABDO, 2009.

ON THE INTERNET

Australia Zoo
http://www.australiazoo.com.au/

Bindi Wear International
http://www.bindiwearinternational.com/

El Hasan, Mariam. "Bindi Irwin Fights for Animals." Scholastic, April 9, 2010. http://blogs.scholastic.com/kidspress/2010/04/bindi-irwin-fights-for-animals.html

WORKS CONSULTED

"A Chat with Bindi." ABC 4 Kids. http://www.abc.net.au/children/bindi/interview.htm

"Bindi Irwin Interview for Free Willy: Escape from Pirate's Cove." http://www.youtube.com/watch?v=EEwoWOsRSaw

Clark, Champ. "Chip Off The Old Croc." *People*, June 18, 2007.

"Rising Star." *Scholastic News*, April 30, 2007.

"Terri Irwin Live Chat Archive." Animal Planet, June 21, 2011. http://animal.discovery.com/fansites/crochunter/chat_archive.html

INDEX